Clayton Family History

From England to Virginia, the Carolinas, Kentucky, Missouri, and Beyond

Melinda Clayton

Clayton Family History

From England to Virginia, the Carolinas,
Kentucky, Missouri, and Beyond

Copyright 2021 Melinda Clayton
Published by Thomas-Jacob Publishing, LLC
TJPub@thomas-jacobpublishing.com

Hardback information:
Library of Congress Control Number: 2021934619
1. Reference/Genealogy and Heraldry 2. Family and Relationships/Reference
ISBN-10: 1-950750-38-8
ISBN-13: 978-1-950750-38-2
Thomas-Jacob Publishing, LLC, Deltona, Florida

First Edition
First Printing: March 2021
Printed in the United States of America

Table of Contents

Introduction

As anyone who's researched Clayton history over the years can tell you, there are a lot of tangled branches to sort through.

This booklet was created for my husband, sons, and in-laws as a labor of love using nearly 70 sources, from books published in the 16-, 17-, 18-, and 1900s, to the online ancestry sites of modern times. All sources used are listed in the Bibliography in the back of the book.

It's as researched, sourced, and accurate as I'm capable of making it. That said, understand that I'm not a genealogist, and this is not meant to be a scholarly work, as some of my asides—not to mention the irreverent comments of my husband—will no doubt demonstrate.

My hope is that readers find information to help them untangle their own branches, and if in that process they find new twigs and leaves I may have overlooked, that's fantastic (and I'd love to know about them). If they find a smile or two along the way, that's even better.

For those picky about citation methods, know that I cited sources using a blend of MLA and Chicago. Each superscript number within the text corresponds to a numbered entry in the Bibliography. This was done deliberately in order to give proper credit where credit is due while also avoiding nearly constant interruptions in the narrative.

Best wishes and happy reading,

Melinda

The Clayton Coat of Arms

Contrary to popular belief, not all families were granted a coat of arms. Those were reserved for individuals who had somehow pleased the Crown, and only those descended from the legitimate male line of the individual granted a coat of arms had the right to use it.[31]

As history would have it, Claytons purportedly all descended from one man (more on him later), and the picture below demonstrates the blazen of arms[27] bestowed upon that man by William the Conqueror in 1066:

Graphic property of the author and released to public domain.

The blazen of arms is the official, written description for a specific coat of arms.[30] As Ralph Toresby told us in 1715, "Clayton

3

bears Argent a Cross engrailed Sable between four Torteauxes" (p. 256).

Argent tells us our shield is silver, or more accurately, the silver color one might see on the night of a full moon.[51] A cross engrailed is a cross with points along the outer edges, with the points representing land and water. Sable tells us our cross is black. Torteaux (plural of torteau) are raised red roundels signifying the bread, generally identified as communion bread, a warrior would eat before going into battle. There are different colors of roundels, each named for its color. Red ones (torteaux) are used to symbolize warriors and military strength.[38]

Aside from the blazen, the artistic rendition of the coat of arms includes a crest,[51] which is the symbol on top of the helmet. Although each crest has a specific meaning, other elements (the helmet, torse, and mantling) are generally not part of the blazen and are left up to the discretion of the artist.

The choice of helmet was dependent on the fashion of the day. The torse is a bolt of cloth wound around the crest to hold it to the helmet. The mantling is a cloak or cape designed not only to protect warriors from the weather, but also to provide some small measure of protection from attack. The torse and mantling, designed for functionality on the battlefield but stylized on artistic renderings, were typically in the colors of the blazen (in your case red, black, and silver).[30]

Different branches of the Clayton family have developed different coats of arms over the centuries, but this one, dating back to the 12th century, represents the first, that of the Lancashire Claytons of Clayton-le-Moors. It has a "dexter arm embowed, the hand grasping a dagger, the point to the dexter, all argent" (Bellarts, p. 4):

A "dexter arm" is an arm bent at the elbow, with the bend appearing on the left side to an observer. "Embowed" indicates it should appear sinister. In regard to the dagger, "the point to the dexter, all argent" means the blade, also appearing on the left to an observer, should be silver.[51]

I think the meaning of this one is pretty clear.

This next one is the one for your specific branch, the Claytons descended from John de Clayton of Clayton Hall. We'll talk more about where you branched off later, but for now:

Graphic property of the author and released to public domain.

Instead of a dagger, yours has "a leopard's gamb, erased and erect" holding a torteau. The gamb is the paw or front leg of the leopard. In heraldry, the leopard (in later years typically represented by a lion) is a symbol of strength, courage, ferocity, and valor, while using the leg specifically indicates strength, stability, and speed.[38]

The Clayton family motto came about in the years after William the Conqueror bestowed the coat of arms. In Latin, it's *Probitatum quam divitias*, which translates roughly into "Integrity rather than riches."[26]

Robert de Clayton: William the Conqueror's Warrior

To fully understand Clayton history, we have to begin with a Viking raider named Rollo, who was descended from the Vikings of Scandinavia. From the late 900s through the early 1000s, Rollo and his fellow Vikings pillaged northern France, ultimately reaching a peace agreement when the King of France, King Charles III the Simple, offered Rollo the territory which would come to be known as Normandy.[59] [Side note: According to Hepburn, King Charles the Simple once toppled off his throne while raising his foot to be kissed, so the nickname "Simple" seems pretty on point. But that's a story for another day].

Anyway, a few generations later William the Conqueror became the seventh duke of Normandy, descendant of Rollo the Viking, and decided to stake his claim to an old promise made by his cousin Edward the Confessor, the king of England. King Edward had reportedly promised the English throne to William, but from his deathbed, Edward reneged on his promise and instead proclaimed Harold Godwineson to be King Harold II of England.

As William prepared his troops to invade England and take the throne he believed was rightfully his, he was accompanied by a French soldier named Robert, son of Hugh and grandson of Leofwine of Normandy. Robert was apparently quite skilled in battle, and William was so appreciative of Robert's service during

7

the Battle of Hastings on October 14, 1066, that he gave Robert a gift: the Manor of Clayton, located in Lancashire.[37] [Side note: William won. They didn't call him the "Conqueror" for nothing.]

How, you might ask, could there have been a Clayton Manor if there hadn't previously been a Clayton? The answer is that it wasn't called Clayton Manor *per se* back then; it was most likely something along the lines of "Claegtun," from "claeg," meaning "clay," and "tun," meaning settlement. In other words, William gave Robert a farmstead on land composed of a clay-like soil.[26]

Clayton Manor, Lancashire, England. Copyright Ian Greig and licensed for reuse under a CC BY- SA 2.0.

Robert was known thereafter as Robert de Clayton (Robert of Clayton). Thus, the first Clayton came to be. Because this is the first known use of the name, it follows that all Claytons have shared DNA at some point down the line, meaning you're all related. But given the many tangled branches formed over nearly

1,000 years of history, you're a long way from being close relatives, or even *detectable* relatives beyond five generations or so.[56]

At various points along the way, the line branched out from those original Lancashire Claytons to include Yorkshire County, Sussex County, Staffordshire County, and beyond, finally crossing the ocean and arriving into the first British colonies of North America. Over the centuries, the name Clayton has also changed numerous times. Clatan, Claiton, Cleton, Cleaton, and Claydon are just a few of the simplest variations.[26]

We're going to trace the history of your specific branch from Lancashire, to Yorkshire, to Virginia, the Carolinas, Kentucky, Missouri, and beyond, but first, a couple of things to keep in mind. Because Europe has had many disasters, including wars both internally and externally, it is, as Henry F. Hepburn lamented, "next to impossible to get the family registry of the various branches" (p. 11). Churches, where births, marriages, and deaths might have been recorded, were often destroyed. Even those records that survived can be very difficult to read due to the language, style of writing, and age.

Add to that the fact that back in the old days, we loved to use the same given names *ad infinitum* in a family. The end result is that it's easy to miss the fourth William, or the seventh John, etc. For that reason, generations are sometimes overlooked, and different branches are often confused. If you notice the dates between fathers and sons being more than a few decades apart, there's a good chance a generation was skipped.

Wives and children, too, are sometimes assigned to the wrong husband and father, if they're recorded at all. Just as men often died young in battle, women often died young in childbirth. There were many remarriages and blended families, and aside from those unions in which women brought inherited land and wealth to their husbands, the lives of women weren't generally recorded. It was the same with children. Unless a child was heir to the family legacy or grew up to do something historically note-worthy, their existence wasn't always recorded, and certainly not by genealogists and historians.

All that said, this is as thorough a direct line as I can make it, thanks to the sources listed in the back. In the two places I can't determine the exact leaf, I can still get you on the branch.

The History of Clayton Manor (and Clayton Hall)

Henry F. Hepburn[37] and James E. Bellarts[21] are two of the most prominent genealogists who've worked on early Clayton history, and they, along with Bill Putnam,[54] are the primary sources used for this section.

A quick word about Bellarts and Hepburn: There was a man named William Clayton who came to North America on a ship named the *Kent* and settled in what would later become Pennsylvania. This William Clayton was allegedly friends with William Penn, for whom Pennsylvania was named. That information has since come into question; it's not clear how well the two men knew each other. Whether they knew each other well or not, there's plenty of evidence that William Clayton was heavily involved in political affairs in the area.

At any rate, Bellarts first drew a link from that William Clayton to one of the Thomas Claytons in our line, and Hepburn repeated that information in his later work. I, too, initially followed that line before learning that many years later, subsequent genealogists disputed the link based on new information. Changing information is normal and to be expected in genealogy (and other historical works) as new information comes to light. All that said, the genealogical work of Bellarts and Hepburn on both the early

Clayton line and other projects has stood the test of time and they remain well-respected in their fields.

And now, back to our previously scheduled program.

Once we get to North America I'll go into more detail with your family history, but I thought it might be interesting for you to see how you connect to those medieval Claytons. As we go through the generations, keep in mind that when possible, the manor always passed to the oldest son, so that's where the emphasis will always be, although in many cases there were no doubt many other children.

I'll summarize based on the above three sources.

1. Robert de Clayton was the original Clayton who was gifted Clayton Manor by William the Conqueror. He was born in Caudebec, Normandy, France sometime around 1030. According to our sources, he was the son of Hugh and grandson of Leofwine of Normandy. He had three sons, the eldest of whom was William.

2. William de Clayton was born in Normandy sometime around 1060. William was actually the younger son, but his older brother was killed in the war against Scotland, so William inherited the manor. William had one son, Robert, before he was also killed in a battle on Candlemass Day, 1141.

3. Robert was born around 1120. He married and had three sons, but only one survived long enough to inherit Clayton Manor, and that was another Robert.

4. Robert had four sons, but three of them (William, Robert, and Thomas) were killed in Normandy while fighting for England in 1200. That left one, John, to inherit the manor.

5. John was born around 1180. He had two sons, but apparently the older son died, because the younger son, Thomas, inherited the manor.

6. Thomas was born around 1210. His oldest son, John, apparently made it long enough to inherit Clayton Manor.

7. John was born around 1240. He married his first cousin and had at least two sons: Thomas and Ralph.

8. Ralph was born around 1260. He had three sons: John, Giles, and Nicholas. The oldest was John.

9. John was born around 1290. He had three sons: John, Richard, and Robert. John inherited the manor.

10. John was born around 1330. He had four sons: John, William, Ralph, and Robert. John inherited the manor.

11. John was born around 1360. He had three sons: Thomas, Robert, and William.

12. Thomas was born around 1390. He had two sons: John and William.

13. John was born around 1419. He first married a woman named Mary Mainwaring and had two sons, Thomas and William, and three daughters before Mary died in 1445. John then married Jane Clifton and had sons Robert and Richard.

The oldest son, Thomas, was disinherited for disobeying his parents. At that time, Thomas' younger brother Richard was chosen to inherit the manor, but both Richard and his brother William died before having children. Since Thomas wasn't allowed to inherit the manor, it went to Thomas' son Robert.

14. Robert was born around 1470. He married Jane Farrington and had four sons: Thomas, John, Edward, and Richard. And, as Putnam says, now we have a split:

A. As the oldest, Robert's son Thomas (born around 1498) inherited Clayton Manor. He married Anne Jackson and had at least two sons, the oldest of whom was Robert.

    i. Robert was the vice Chancellor of Cambridge. He married and had a son named John.

        ii. John had two daughters and a son named Richard.

            iii. Richard fell from a horse and died before he had children, so the manor went to the oldest daughter, who was Dorothy.

                iv. Dorothy married George Leycester of Toft, and George sold the manor. ("Bastard!" says my husband.)

B. John (born around 1499) decided to leave and go to Yorkshire, where he founded Clayton Hall. If you can't inherit a manor, by God, go build one yourself.

John had two sons: Thomas, and Richard. The oldest was Thomas.

    i. Thomas married Anguis Thornhill, and they had three sons: John, William (we'll come back to him in a minute), and Thomas. The oldest was John.

        ii. John married a woman whose last name was Barnaby. They had one son: Thomas.

iii. Thomas married Alice Burdette, and they sold Clayton Hall to Sir George Cook of Wheatly. ("What the hell!" says my husband.)

Although there were no more direct heirs to either Clayton Manor or Clayton Hall, the lines continued, of course, with many graduates of Cambridge including doctors, lawyers, and rectors—not the "I got drunk on Saturday and saved on Sunday" kind of rector, but the "I earned my Doctor of Divinity degree from Cambridge" kind of rector.

I wanted to show you where and how Clayton Manor and Clayton Hall, the places themselves, ended up, but there's a lot more to say about John of Clayton Hall because this is where we'll find Samuel.

John de Clayton (1499) son of Robert de Clayton

When John decided to leave Clayton Manor in 1540 and build Clayton Hall, he apparently decided to leave the "de" behind, as well, according to Putnam, because from that point on, he's plain old John Clayton.

There seems to be quite a bit of information on various sites these days that confuses Clayton Manor with Clayton Hall. For example, *Wikipedia* states that, "The oldest section of the remaining wing of Clayton Hall was built in the 15th century on the site of a 12th-century house built for the Clayton family."[25]

Hepburn, Putnam, and other valid sources are clear, though, that John de Clayton founded Clayton Hall in *Yorkshire* around 1540, while Clayton Manor in *Lancashire*, which wasn't only a home but also an estate, was given to Robert in 1066. I can only assume *Wikipedia* and other online sites have confused the two. Or maybe I'm confused. But in this case, anyway, I don't think so.

Surrounded by an actual moat, John's Clayton Hall still exists today, albeit with many changes of hands and restorations over the years. Although the history is confused and confusing, it's now being restored once again to be converted into a "Hands-on Living History Museum."[25]

16

Photo copyright Keith Williamson, 2005. CC BY-SA 2.0

It's also supposed to be haunted by a boggart, or poltergeist, who likes to rattle chains, drag things across floors, and yank on bed-clothes. There's even a little poem: "Whilst ivy climbs and holly is green/Clayton Hall Boggart shall no more be seen."[66]

Maybe it's John, and he's angry that no one seems to remember where Clayton Hall came from. I would be. First, he didn't inherit the manor, then he built his own hall, and now people can't keep it straight.

Moving on, you may find this map handy as we start to talk about John's (your) branch:

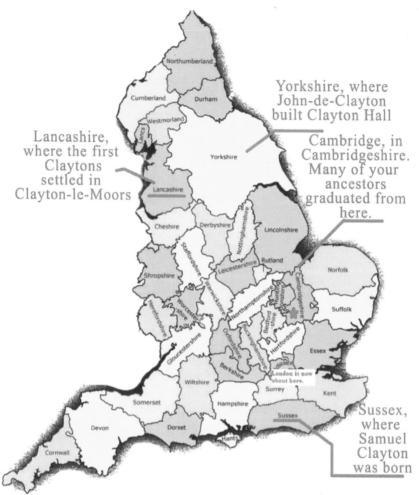

Lancashire, where the first Claytons settled in Clayton-le-Moors

Yorkshire, where John-de-Clayton built Clayton Hall

Cambridge, in Cambridgeshire. Many of your ancestors graduated from here.

Northumberland

Cumberland   Durham

Westmorland

Lancs

Yorkshire

Lancashire

Cheshire   Derbyshire

Nottinghamshire   Lincolnshire

Staffordshire

Shropshire   Warwickshire   Leicestershire   Rutland

Norfolk

Herefordshire   Worcestershire   Northamptonshire   Huntingdonshire   Cambridgeshire   Suffolk

Gloucestershire   Oxfordshire   Buckinghamshire   Bedfordshire   Hertfordshire   Essex

Berkshire   London is now about here.

Wiltshire   Surrey   Kent

Somerset   Hampshire

Devon   Dorset   Sussex

Hants

Cornwall

Sussex, where Samuel Clayton was born

Map from Wikimedia Commons and in the public domain.

Hepburn and Putnam indicate that the wife of John of Clayton Hall is unknown, but other sources include up to three wives. Sources also disagree on how many children he had. Hepburn and Putnam, however, agree on the two mentioned previously: Richard and Thomas.

As stated earlier, Thomas (1525) married a woman named Anguis Thornhill and had three sons: John, William, and Thomas. You already know about John, whose son sold Clayton Hall. Not much is mentioned about Thomas; in fact, Hepburn doesn't mention him at all, and Putnam gives him William's wife.

It's William we're interested in.

We've been using Hepburn and Putnam as resources and we'll continue to do that, but for Scenario 1 here we're also throwing in *The Visitation of the County of Yorke*, by William Dugdale, Esquire, published in 1666,[29] and *A History of Northumberland in Three Parts, Vol. 2-3*, by John Hodgson-Hinde, published in 1840.[40]

Scenario 1

I. William (b. unknown, d. 1627) was a lawyer, or Barrister at Law, and he married Margaret Cholmeley, the daughter of another lawyer. They had eight sons and three daughters. Dugdale lists only one son, but Hepburn, Hodgson-Hinde, and Putnam list four of the eight:

> **A.** William, of whom there's no record;
> **B.** Thomas, who moved to London and had 5 sons and 2 daughters, none of them named by our sources;
> **C.** Sir Jasper Clayton, whom we'll talk more about later; and
> **D.** John, whom we'll talk about now.

II. John (1592-1671) was also a Barrister at Law. He had at least two wives, and possibly three, all of whom were named Elizabeth (in no particular order, because I don't know the order: Citterne, Fitzwilliam, and Eceleston). Hepburn, Hodgson-Hinde, and Dugdale list only two sons, but given that he had 2-3 wives, I think it's quite likely there were many more; these are just the ones our sources deemed historically significant:

> **A.** John (b. 1620), another Barrister at Law, who died without children, and

B. James (b. 1624), who became a Doctor of Divinity. Hepburn tells us his descendants produced many ministers and lawyers, but none of them are named.

And here's where it gets a little tricky. Many online family trees have *a* John as being the father of our Samuel, but they often have birth and death dates, wife/wives, siblings, and locations mixed up betwixt and between all the many Johns along all the various Clayton branches.

Hepburn believed our Samuel came from this branch, and we'll talk about that more in a minute. But for now, we have another source, a Dr. Mel R. Brashears,[23] who is literally a rocket scientist. His bio describes him as:

> "Retired as President and Chief Operating Officer of Lockheed Martin's Space and Strategic Missiles Sector. Also served as Co-Chairman of the Board with United Space Alliance operations of the Space Shuttle for NASA. In addition, was Chairman of the Board of Space Imaging, Inc., world's first one-meter commercial system. Oversaw more than 275 launches and space events during career. PhD University of Missouri."

Dr. Brashears has studied the genealogy of all sides of his family, over 3,000 ancestors, and he believes John (1592-1671) and one of his Elizabeths (Citterne, according to Dr. Brashears) had another son:

C. Samuel.

I've spent months studying every single lead, all the Johns, Henrys, Alexanders, and other men said to be Samuel's father, from this branch to the original Lancashire Branch and all across England—even to a tiny little parish in Aldingham, next to the Irish

Sea—and all of that research has led me to agree with Dr. Brashears. I believe John (1592-1671) and one of his Elizabeth's—maybe Citterne—to be the parents of our Samuel.

Unfortunately, my emails have gone unanswered, and I suspect Dr. Brashears may no longer be online because he stopped his research with John and Elizabeth (he doesn't make it back any further than that) and all of his social media accounts have been silent since 2016. I would have loved to talk with him, but it doesn't look as if I'll get the chance.

And that brings us to Scenario 2.

Scenario 2

To recap:

I. William (b. unknown, d. 1627) was a lawyer, or Barrister at Law, and he married Margaret Cholmeley, the daughter of another lawyer. They had eight sons and three daughters. Dugdale lists only one son, but Hepburn, Hodgson-Hinde, and Putnam list four of the eight:

> **A.** William, of whom there's no record;
> **B.** Thomas, who moved to London and had 5 sons and 2 daughters, none of them named by our sources;
> **C.** John, whom we've just talked about, and
> **D.** Sir Jasper, whom we'll talk about now.

For this scenario we're using Hepburn, and within his research, he mentions Phillip Slaughter's *History of Culpepper County*.

II. Sir Jasper married Mary Thompson in 1624. He was an alderman of London (part of the senior governance) and was knighted at Guildhall in 1660. He and Mary had two sons:

A. George, and

B. John, whom we'll talk about now.

III. Jasper's son John was a Barrister at Law, and he was also knighted in 1664. He married and had a son named John in 1665.

IV. John Jr. (1665) was also a Barrister at Law. His wife is unknown. John immigrated to Virginia in 1705 and was appointed Attorney General of the British colony in 1714. He held that office until he died in 1737. This John had at least three sons:

A. Thomas (1701-1739), who was a Cambridge-educated doctor. He died in Gloucester County, Virginia at the age of 39, and the Clayton blazen of arms, along with the leopard's (or lion's) paw, is engraved in his tomb, which can be found at Warner Hall Cemetery in Gloucester County, Virginia. The site is now under the protection of Preservation Virginia.[65]

Graphic property of the author and released to public domain.

B. Arthur, who was also involved in governance, and

C. John (1685-1783), who also went to Cambridge and became a doctor and famous botanist known the western world over.[37] He wrote several books regarding planting and fertilization methods that were considered ground-breaking for their time (no pun intended).[53]

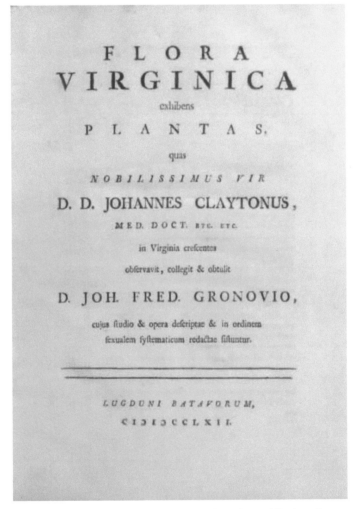

John was also the clerk of Gloucester County for over 50 years, from 1720-1772. In 1951, the Virginia State Library erected a historical marker north of Virginia State Route 14, which is also known as John Clayton Memorial Highway. The sign directs travelers to the site of his old plantation, which he named Windsor.[53]

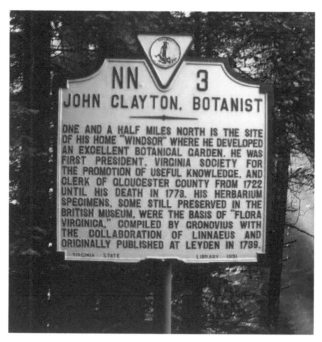

Graphic property of the author and released to public domain.

Hepburn speculates John the Attorney General also had a fourth son, brother to Thomas, Arthur, and John:

D. Samuel.

In many ways, the speculation makes sense; Samuel, too, came from Sussex around the same time, and he was in the same area of Virginia at the same time as John the Attorney General and his sons.

The problem is, we know from the genealogy of other families, specifically the Pendleton family (more on that later) that Samuel was born around 1640. John the Attorney General's other sons were born 45-60 years after Samuel, which indicates to me there's a generation, more likely two, skipped in this scenario.

My legitimate sources and I all agree he came from this line; the disagreement is in regard to who his father may have been. Either way, you know you're a part of the Sussex County group of Claytons who descended from John Clayton of Clayton Hall. Dr. Brashears and I just think you're a couple of generations closer to him than Hepburn thought.

Now that we've finally got Samuel, we'll pick up with the Clayton line in Virginia.

The Claytons Come to America

When speculating that Samuel was the son of John Clayton, Attorney General of Virginia, Hepburn wrote, "[I]t appears by Slaughter's *History of Culpepper County*, that Samuel Clayton, of New Kent, who is supposed to be a son of John Clayton, the Attorney-General of Virginia, married Elizabeth Pendleton, a daughter of Philip Pendleton ..." (17). This is further indication that Putnam missed a generation or two.

Our first Samuel didn't marry a Pendleton; our second one did. So that I don't have to repeatedly interrupt the narrative below with sources, the history of our two Samuels and their marriages and children comes from the following places: Ancestry.com birth, marriage, and burial databases (all listed in the Bibliography); John Boddie's *Historical Southern Families*;[22] G. Watson James' *Sons of the Revolution in State of Virginia Quarterly Magazine*, Volumes 1-2;[41] *Historical and Biographical Papers*, Volume 4, Issues 34-42;[39] and Yates Publishing marriage database 1560-1900.[69]

III. Samuel Clayton (1640-1702) was born in Sussex, England. There were several Samuel Claytons recorded arriving into Virginia in the late 1600s, so we can't be sure which one was him, but we can be sure that once he got there, he married Susannah Morris. They settled in Gloucester County, Virginia and had at least the following children:

   A. Morris (unknown)

B. Thomas (birth date unknown, died about 1670)

C. John (1675 - 1737), whom we'll talk about next,

D. Jeremy (unknown), and we'll talk about him, too.

E. Samuel Jr., who married Elizabeth Pendleton. The Pendleton family has done a great deal of genealogical research, which helped me find our Samuel from the bottom up. Samuel Jr. and Elizabeth had a son named Phillip—Major Phillip Clayton—who reportedly formed and headed a militia to fight in the Revolutionary War.

IV. John (1675-1737) ... or possibly Jeremy. The history here once again gets a little interesting, because Dr. Brashears, whom I mentioned earlier, has Jeremy listed as your direct ancestor instead of John.

I hesitate to move away from Brashears, but I can find no evidence that this is the case, either within Brashears' information or without. According to Brashears, Jeremy was born in 1683 and married a woman named Margaret Poteet. Brashears says they had the following children: Jeremiah (1700), John (1702), Daniel (1705), and William (1710). He says that Jeremy died in 1712 at the age of 29 in Gloucester County, Virginia.

Historian John Boddie tells us that in 1704 both Jeremy and John owned several hundred acres next to the several hundred their mother, Susannah, inherited from their father Samuel, so we know Jeremy was alive then. But Dr. Brashears doesn't include any sources for this section, and aside from Boddie's brief mention, I simply can't find anything else about Jeremy. I can't even find a woman named Margaret Poteet (or even Petit or Petite) from the right time and place in any database or publication.

It's possible Dr. Brashears has information about Jeremy I don't have access to, perhaps information directly from his family that may not be published or contained in the usual databases. For example, he has DNA results posted on his website which no doubt provide information I don't have, and maybe that information has led him to Jeremy.

But without more information, I have to go with what I can source, which is Boddie's *Historical Southern Families* (1957). Boddie tells us that Jeremy's brother John married a woman named Mary Saddler, and they had at least the following children:

A. John
B. Rebecca (b. 1696),
C. George (1698-1767),
D. William

Quite a few online family trees indicate John had many more children, some of them stepchildren, including a Daniel and/or a Jeremiah. If John's brother Jeremy did indeed die young, it's possible John raised, or at least helped to raise, Jeremy's children—children who, according to Brashears, included a Jeremiah and a Daniel. But again, we just don't know.

Whether John's son or Jeremy's son, it's William, grandson of Samuel, that we need.

From Virginia to the Carolinas

To understand our sources for the next section, it might be helpful to see what the area looked like during Colonial times. Prior to 1663, the land making up the Carolinas was part of the colony of Virginia. From 1663-1710, the area below Virginia was known as the Province of Carolina, and it stretched from south of Daytona Beach to what's now the Virginia-North Carolina Border, and from the Atlantic to what is now Tennessee.[24] This is essentially what it would have looked like:

One of the things I noticed when researching your family history was that around 1740 or so, there was a huge movement of not only Claytons, but also Pendletons, Lambs, Brashears, Gowens, Yanceys, and other family names familiar to me by now, all migrating from Virginia into the Carolinas. I knew members from each family had married into the other ones, but it still seemed strange that these huge families were all moving at the same time.

But as I learned more about the area (and U.S. history), it made sense. In 1663 Charles II, king of England, Scotland, and Ireland, granted the Province of Carolina to eight men who were referred to as the "Lord Proprietors." The Lords were given power to create local governments, maintain order, and collect rents and taxes. Given the massive land area and dangerous conditions (including battles with Native American tribes), it proved to be more than most of the Lords wanted to deal with, so over the next 60 or so years, seven of the eight Lord Proprietors sold their land back to the English government. The descendant of one of the original Lords, John Carteret, had inherited the title Earl of Granville from his grandfather along with the northern half of what is now North Carolina. From 1748-1763 in the area of what would become Granville, North Carolina, Lord Carteret's agents performed surveys for settlers and facilitated the sale of land for prices lower than their neighbors to the north.[52]

The Claytons were farmers by this point, primarily tobacco farmers, and they would have wanted as much land as it was possible to farm. They were one of many families who took advantage of that opportunity, many of whom brought slaves along with them from the north.[33]

When it comes to researching family history, South Carolina doesn't make it easy. It wasn't until 1911 that South Carolina was even legally required to record marriages.[60] But it's more than that. Whether from corruption, incompetence, hurricanes, floods, or General William T. Sherman's love of burning down courthouses, the records of South Carolina have been destroyed over and over again throughout the generations.[47]

Once we're through South Carolina and into Kentucky I can use census reports and marriage records, but for our first two Williams, we're primarily working with tax records and land transactions. If it weren't for those, we'd have a hard time following the trail.

We left off with John's son William, who was born in the early 1700s in Gloucester County, Virginia. The first indication that William is in North Carolina is a 1754 land grant for 275 acres on both sides of Jonathan's Creek.[17]

No. *145*

County *Granville*

Name *Clayton William*

Acres *275*

Grant No. *162*

Issued *26 April 1754*

Warrant No. .... Entry No. ....

Entered ....

Book No. *11* Page No. *336*

Location *Lying on both sides of Jonathans Creek*

We can also find William in military records, where he's listed as having served in the Granville County, North Carolina militia with Captain John Sallis' Company.[49] Interestingly, a Jeremiah Clayton is listed as well. A cousin? A brother? It's impossible to know.

There are no marriage records for William, but an Elizabeth is named on some of the land deals along with William, so it's a fairly good bet she was his wife.

V. William Clayton Sr. and his wife, probably Elizabeth, had at least one son and probably more:

   A. William Jr. (1740-1807), who is present on some of those land deals either as a witness, or as a partner.

William Sr. and Elizabeth's land transactions continue, both buying and selling, until 1762, when they sell 100 acres on both sides of Jonathan's Creek to a man named Thornton Yancey. This transaction was witnessed by William Jr. One of the stipulations made is that William Sr. and Elizabeth be allowed to live there for the rest of their natural lives.[18] William Sr., at least, would have been around sixty at that time.

VI. William Jr.'s first wife is listed on some of his land transactions as Betty, and Dr. Brashers lists his wife as Elizabeth Yancey. I can't find a record of that marriage, but it's possible, even likely, since Yanceys were also in the area and involved in various transactions with Claytons.

The following children are the ones most commonly attached to William Jr. and Betty on various online genealogy sites:

   A. Moses (1761-1836). We'll talk about him in a minute.

B. William (1774-1845)
C. Elizabeth (1781-1857)
D. Catherine

According to Dr. Brashears, there were also:

E. John
F. Francis
G. James
H. Edmond

There are multiple appearances of all of those names (John, Francis, James, Edmond) and more (Daniel, Jeremiah, Gowan, Isham) in various transactions, and they may all be the children of William. It's just impossible to know. Moses is the one who seems to be involved most frequently either in land transactions with his father or as a witness to transactions between other parties. Or maybe that's simply because he's the one I've researched the most.

There are other Claytons in the area, too, who are almost certainly related: Augustine Absalom, retired Revolutionary War soldier-turned-minister; John, his brother who was his commanding officer; Elizabeths, Sarahs; Rebeccas; Marys; and Sirrah (Sarah) Hatcher, who married a different John Clayton and gave birth to more Claytons named John, William, and Isham.

(In online family trees poor Sirrah has been attached to every Clayton man on both sides of the ocean, but records kept by Reverend John Giessendanner known as *The Giessendanner Church Record-Book* make it clear Sirrah, widow of John Fuster,[60] was married to John Clayton in Orangeburg in 1741/42. See, Sirrah? I told you I'd set the record straight. Rest easy now.)

Anyway, suffice it to say, the Carolinas were apparently saturated with Claytons.[34]

Other family records, such as genealogy from the Gowen family, even capture some of the many transactions occurring between Claytons themselves, and between Claytons and other families.[36] Land passed from [Unknown] Clayton to John Clayton to William Clayton to Moses Clayton—and then signed by Moses and witnessed by Isham—is typical of some of the entries I've seen.

But back to William Jr. In 1769, he received the first of several "Royal grants" for acres in what is now Spartanburg, South Carolina. The first, in 1769, was for 250 acres. The second, in 1772, was for 200 acres. One in 1774 was for another 250 acres, and a second was for 200 acres. Both of those were for land along the Tyger River. The last, in 1775, was for yet another 250 acres.[17]

He also served in the Revolutionary War as a sergeant in Benjamin Roebuck's militia unit after the fall of Charleston May 12, 1780[58] and was paid for his service, but for some reason turned it over to a man named Samuel Farrow:[57]

[p 2]
[No.] 3438   No. 114   3438 X
[Book] X   2nd of August 86 [1786]
William Clayton Sergeant For Militia Duty in Roebuck's [Benjamin Roebuck's] Regiment, since the fall of Charleston [Charleston South Carolina fell to the British on May 12, 1780] per Henderson's [Colonel Robert Anderson's] Return [not extant] Amounting to
        [old South Carolina] Currency   £32.10
                            Sterling   £4.12.10 ¼
Exd. J. Mc. A. G. [Examined by John McCall, Adjutant General]

Received 2nd of August 1786 full Satisfaction for the within in an Indent No. 3438 X, per order
                S/ Saml. Farrow [Samuel Farrow]

[Illegible]
Messrs. Boquet & Mitchal Treasury Keepers Gentlemen please to deliver to Mr. Samuel Farrow my indents and my Special indents and this my order shall be your Receipt for the same. Witness my hand this 17th July 1786
S/ Spencer Bobo Witness   S/ William Clayton

[p 5: Printed form of Indent No. 3438 Book X dated August 2nd, 1786]

I've wondered if he was paying for even more land, but I didn't find any records to clarify.

Ten years later, William Jr. married his second wife, Nancy Roberts, in Madison, Kentucky on December 4, 1796.[15] This would have been four years after Kentucky was admitted to the Union and just as settlers were flooding the area and introducing tobacco, corn, and hemp as the major crops.

William Jr.'s son Moses also ends up in Kentucky, and we'll talk about him next.

From Moses (1761–1836) to Jesse James (1793–1856)

I must admit, after having nothing but land and tax records to go on for the past two ancestors, I've been looking forward to telling you about Moses.

There are no records for his first marriage, but the general consensus among both the Clayton and Lamb lines seems to be that he first married Phoebe Lamb.

The Lambs were one of the families moving right along with the Claytons from Virginia to the Carolinas, and then into Kentucky. One point I found interesting is that the Lamb family, Phoebe's parents and eight siblings, were Quakers, but apparently a few of them struggled with abiding by the rules.

Phoebe's oldest brother, Thomas Jr., was disowned for an "indiscretion" with a woman. Another brother, Longshore, was disowned for marrying a woman not a Quaker. And then there was Phoebe, who was disowned by the Quakers after much intervention and prayer, for "going to a disorderly marriage, she being treated with and not appearing in a capacity to make suitable satisfaction."[20] Poor Phoebe. Those Clayton men will do that to you.

But back to Moses.

VII. Moses (1761 – 1836) and Phoebe had at least the following children:

    A. Wiley (1790)
    B. Jesse (1793-1850), and we'll talk about him later.
    C. William (1794-1856)
    D. Mary Polly (1797-1864)
    E. John Gowan (1798)
    F. Francis (1803-1866)

The census of 1800 shows that Moses was living in Madison County, Kentucky, along with his father,[14] but the censuses of 1810[1] and 1820[2] show Moses and family in Caldwell, Kentucky, where he was a busy man.

Moses wasn't only a landowner and a farmer; he was also a businessman. On April 28, 1818, Moses petitioned the Caldwell County Court to obtain a one-year license to open a tavern in his house. He listed his son Francis Clayton as his security (this means "co-signer" or "bondsman" instead of actual bar security, although I have no doubt he could have served as bouncer if the need arose), and paid a £100 fee and an annual tax.[43]

This wasn't quite the wild west. There were strict laws that had to be followed. For example, Moses had to promise not to allow gaming (gambling) in his tavern or to "'suffer any person to tipple or drink more than is necessary,' or permit scandalous behavior." Failure to abide by those promises could result in a fine, closure of the tavern, and/or seizure of the liquor.[44]

On February 10, 1819, Moses filed "Articles of Partnership" to own and run a mercantile business with a man named Edward C. Bearden.[42] If you look at our source, number 42 on the Bibliography page, you'll see a link that will take you to the website to see the actual document Moses signed.

He was also active in the community and was often called on to appraise estates or survey land and building projects. For example, on April 27, 1818, Moses was appointed surveyor over a portion of the public road "leading from Hopkinsville to Centreville commencing at the county line," and he, his son Jesse, and a crew of other men were responsible for keeping the road in good condition.[43]

Some of Moses' dealings and interactions involved Phoebe's brother Longshore, too. For example, on July 17, 1818, Moses, Longshore Lamb, and a man named William Crow were "in the service of the court to settle an estate in Caldwell County, Kentucky."[45]

By the census of 1830, Moses Clayton had wandered on to Union, Kentucky. Back in those days, the only names listed on the census were those of the head of household, but 9 other people are noted to have been present in the home: four under the age of 20 (2 males, 2 females), 3 ages 20-49 (1 male, 2 females), one female between the ages of 50-59, and one male between the ages of 60-69.[3] That would have been Moses, who would have been around 69 by then.

I don't know why Moses relocated to Union, but one reason might have been his new wife, Nancy. Her maiden name is unknown, but she was the widow of a William Blackwell. The marriage was witnessed by Moses's son Jesse on February 4, 1830[15] (see next page):

Know all men by these presents that we Moses Clayton and Jesse Clayton are held and firmly bound unto the Commonwealth of Kentucky in the penal sum of Fifty pounds current money to the payment of which well and truly to be made to the said Commonwealth we bind ourselves our heirs Executors and administrators Jointly and severally firmly by these presents sealed with our seals and dated this 8th day of February 1830.

The condition of the above obligation is such that whereas there is a marriage shortly intended between the above bound Moses Clayton and Mrs Nancy Blackwell widow of William Blackwell deceased if there be no lawful just cause to prevent an obstruct said marriage Then this obligation to be void otherwise to remain in full force and virtue in law

[signatures]

VII. Jesse (1793-1850), son of Moses, is referred to in some places as Jesse James. Jesse is listed on his son's death certificate as having been born in Virden, Illinois, but I suspect this was because his *son* was born in Illinois so it was assumed Jesse had been, too. But it's much more likely Jesse was born in Caldwell, Kentucky, where he also met and married his first wife.

That was Jensey "Jane" Lamb, and they married in Caldwell, Kentucky on October 18, 1811.[15]

Jensey Jane Lamb was the daughter of Longshore Lamb, whom you may remember was the brother of Phoebe Lamb, Moses' wife.[45] In other words, Jesse married his first cousin, which actually wasn't unusual back then. In fact, I've come across several instances of cousins marrying just in this family history alone.

The 1820[2] census has Jesse living in Caldwell with four female children under the age of ten. By 1830,[3] he's living in Calloway, Kentucky, and the census lists five female children and one male child.

Online family trees list several children, all some combination of Elizabeth B. (1812), Sarah (1817), Phoebe (1819), Mary Ann (1820), Moses (1821), John S. (1827), and William P. (1832).

Shortly after this census, records show that Jesse left Kentucky for Illinois, where he's listed as having served in Captain Walter Butler's regiment in the Black Hawk War in Illinois in 1831-32.[19]

Sauk leader Black Hawk had crossed the Mississippi with a band of Sauk, Meskwaki, and Kickapoo Native Americans ostensibly hoping to resettle on tribal lands that had been taken by the U.S. government in the Treaty of St. Louis of 1804. According to *Wikipedia*, "Black Hawk's motives were ambiguous, but he was apparently hoping to avoid bloodshed."[62] Of course, bloodshed was not avoided.

For Jesse's service, he was granted 40 acres in Franklin County, Illinois, but on February 6, 1854, he assigned the patent over to a woman named Elizabeth Ewing.[35] I'd love to know the story here, but I haven't been able to find out who she was. I can't help but wonder if this was his daughter Elizabeth, but I haven't been able to find proof.

Jesse spends several years in Illinois,[13] returning to Kentucky in 1837, when he marries his second wife, Elizabeth (alternately

Betsy or Bettie) Parrish, on October 19, 1837.[15] He's living in Union at this point, where he's listed in the 1840 census.[4]

By the time we reach the 1850 census,[5] we're seeing the names and ages of those in the home as well as the location and occupation of the head of household:

Jesse [James] Clayton
Gender: Male
Age: 57
Birth Year: 1793
Home in 1850: Union, Kentucky, USA
Occupation: Farmer
Household Members:
Jesse Clayton Age 57
Elizabeth [Betsy] Parrish Clayton Age 36
William P Clayton Age 18
S J [Serena James, according to other sources] Clayton Age 11
Hiram Starling Clayton Age 8
Olive R Clayton Age 6
Andrew Clayton Age 4
H [Helen] T Clayton Age 1, who died in childhood.

With the exception of William P., the children listed as belonging to Jesse and Jensey Jane would have been grown and gone by this point. Serena James, Hiram Starling, Olive R., Andrew, and Helen T. would have belonged to Jesse and his second wife, Elizabeth.

It's Hiram Starling we'll talk about next.

ℱrom Ħiram Starling (1842~1921) to the Present

Ħiram Starling Clayton was born on August 10, 1842. Interestingly, his death certificate, based on information from his son, states he was born in 1832 instead of 1842, but this doesn't match with census reports or other documentation.

Photo from the family.

VIII. Hiram Starling Clayton married a woman named Anna Hatley, sometimes recorded as Hateley, on July 25, 1861 in Webster, Kentucky, when he was nineteen years old.[15]

When the Civil War began Kentucky formally declared neutrality, but that didn't protect the state from bloody battles fought on its soil. We know that Hiram Starling, who was not a member of the military, joined a volunteer regiment, "8 Miscl. [Miscellaneous] U.S. Vols. [Volunteers]," but because he was a volunteer, it's not clear which regiment he fought with, or even where the battles were fought. We do know he filed for his pension under the "Invalid" class on December 11, 1913, which makes one wonder if he was injured in the war:[67]

			(3-H-3)
NAME OF SOLDIER:	*Clayton, Hiram S.*		
NAME OF DEPENDENT:	Widow, Minor,		
SERVICE:	*8 Miscl. U. S. Vols.*		

DATE OF FILING.	CLASS.	APPLICATION NO.	CERTIFICATE NO.	STATE FROM WHICH FILED.
1913 Dec. 11	Invalid,	1.412.560.		Mo.
	Widow,			
	Minor,			
ATTORNEY:	*John W. Morris.*			
REMARKS:				

From *Shotguns Home of the American Civil War*:[61]

[T]he Civil War seriously disrupted the South's tobacco growing and manufacturing. The tobacco-rich states of Virginia, North Carolina, and Tennessee sided with the Confederacy; the success of their crop rose and fell with that of the rebel nation. The tobacco-producing border states of Missouri, Kentucky, and Maryland fell early to Union control. Under the pressure of war, tobacco manufacturing, located in the South throughout the antebellum period, shifted quickly to the North. New York City became the North's tobacco-manufacturing center, servicing the area once dominated by Virginia tobacco planters.

I'm not able to find Hiram for the next few years, but the 1880 census shows him in Missouri:[6]

Hiram [transcribed as "Hirom"] Clayton
Age: 37
Birth Date: About 1843
Birthplace: Kentucky
Home in 1880: Virginia, Pemiscot, Missouri, USA
Dwelling Number: 7
Race: White
Gender: Male
Relation to Head of House: Self
Marital Status: Married
Spouse's Name: Ann Claton
Father's Birthplace: Virginia
Mother's Birthplace: Kentucky
Occupation: Works on Farm
Household members:
Hirom Claton 37 Self
Ann Claton 45 Wife
Gilbert Claton 16 Son
Lyhue Claton 15 Son
Nancy Claton 12 Daughter
John [Richard] Claton 10 Son
William Claton 5 Son

Hiram Starling died February 18, 1921, and was buried in White Cemetery, Pemiscot County, Missouri:[48]

IX. John Richard Clayton, son of Hiram Starling and Anna Hatley, was born in Kentucky on January 6, 1870, but moved to Missouri as a young boy.

He married Almedia (alternately spelled Alameda or Allmedia) Vaughn in Little [original wording "Sutle"] Prairie Township, Pemiscot, Missouri on June 11, 1890.[15]

They had the following children:

    A. James L. (1896)

B. Jessie C [Corbett] (1897)
C. Sidney Clayton (1901)
D. Elva Clayton (1904)
E. Alva Clayton (1904)
F. Gertie Clayton (1908)

Photo from the family.
Front: Gertie
Second row from left to right: Alva, Elva, Sidney
Middle: Jessie Corbett
Back row from left to right: Almedia, John Richard, James L.

It's not clear why Hiram Starling moved to Missouri, but what is clear is that although much of the tobacco industry moved north after the war, the timber industry was booming, with lumbermen entering the Ozarks of southern Missouri and northern Arkansas shortly after the Civil War.

From Milton Rafferty's "The Ozark Forest":[55]

> To nineteenth century Ozarkers trees were both a hindrance and a universal resource. They cut them and burned them to clear land for crops. They hewed them into railroad ties, which were then tied into rafts, and floated downriver to railheads. They sawed them into lumber to be railroaded to distant markets. They built their houses of logs, furnished them and heated them with wood. Bridges were built of timbers and planking. They dammed streams with logs to develop water power to saw lumber, to grind grain and to forge tools. They traveled in wooden boats and wooden wagons, tilled their fields with wooden plows, and most of their tools and household utensils were fashioned from sturdy oak and hickory (23).

Although the 1900 census lists John R.'s occupation as farmer,[7] by 1910 he was living in Little River, Pemiscot, Missouri, and his occupation was listed as "cabiner" at a "box factory," which was transcribed at some point as "Teaming Industry Loading Saw Logs."[8]

He was renting a home at the time of the 1910 census, but by 1930 he owned a home in Lunsford, Poinsett, Arkansas. For some odd reason, the 1930 census also asked if he owned a radio (he didn't).[10]

John Richard passed away on May 27, 1938 at Methodist Hospital in Memphis, Tennessee and was buried in Rowe Cemetery in Wardell, Pemiscot, Missouri.

X. Jessie Corbett Clayton, son of John Robert and Almeda Clayton, was born February 4, 1897 in Pascola, Pemiscot County, Missouri.

The 1920 census lists him as a "teamster" in the "woods industry," which means he would have driven the team of horses or mules—or later, trucks—used to pull the sleigh of logs down to the river or up to the train, wherever the logs were being taken for farther transport.[9]

By this time, the logging industry in the Ozark region was on the downside of its peak. The pine was gone, mills were closing, and lumber companies struggled to sell land that had been overcut, over-burned, and over-grazed.[52]

Photo from the family. Jessie Corbett is on the right.

At the time of the 1930 census, Jessie Corbett's occupation was listed as fireman, and also states that he worked in the cotton gin industry. He was living in Wardell, Missouri and married to Myrtle Lee Haynes.[10]

Their children (and grandchildren) were:

1. Edward Haynes
    A. Billy
    B. Larry
    C. Gary

2. J.C.
    A. Kenny

3. Lennis, who died in infancy, and

4. Mary Francis
  A. Reggie
  B. Jenna

The 1940 census doesn't include Lennis, who had passed away, but does include Mary Francis, who is listed as age 1. Edward Haynes is 16 by then, and J.C. is 14. Jessie Corbett's occupation at that time is deputy sheriff in Wardell, Missouri. He stated he worked 52 weeks per year, and earned an income of $300.[11]

Jessie Corbett was also the constable of Little River Township, a township located in Pemiscot County, Missouri that even now only has a population of 973, according to City-Data.com, and comprises a land area of under 52 square miles.[46]

The July 23, 1940 edition of *The Democrat-Argus* newspaper details an arrest made by "Corbett Clayton, constable of Little River township" when a local man, Jesse Byrd, shot Wade Tucker, the former sheriff of New Madrid County and current representative of the Southern Tenant Farmers Union (which is unfortunately—or maybe hilariously—abbreviated as S.T.F.U.).[68]

I can't include the whole article due to copyright restrictions, but the link to the article in its entirety is in the Bibliography in the back of this book (number 68), and I can include this snippet:

> Corbett Clayton, constable of Little River township, said yesterday that witnesses said the shooting occurred while Tucker was making a militant speech in behalf of the S. T. F. U.

Tucker's "militant" speech was in front of Byrd's Restaurant and Pool Hall in Peach Orchard, and Byrd asked him to move off the property. Tucker refused, then jumped out of the back of his truck and shoved Byrd to the ground. Byrd pulled a pistol from his pocket and shot Tucker twice.

The article says Byrd voluntarily surrendered to Clayton, who filed charges of assault with intent to kill. Byrd was released on a $500 bond while awaiting the hearing.

Jessie Corbett was married for the second time on July 31, 1940 to Grace (listed as Gracie) Chappell. Jessie was 43 at that time, and Grace was 27.[15]

Jessie Corbett Clayton and Grace Chappell Clayton. Photo from the family.

Jessie Corbett Clayton and Grace Chappell Clayton. Photo from the family.

Jessie Corbett Clayton died on June 11, 1965, and was buried in Wardell Memorial Cemetery. Grace Chappell Clayton died October 10, 1985 and was buried in Dunklin Memorial Gardens.

In order to protect privacy, I won't go into detail regarding the rest of this family line, all of whom are living at the time of this writing. Instead, I'll provide a snapshot devoid of spouses, dates, and locations. The children, grandchildren, and great-grandchildren of Jessie Corbett Clayton and Grace Chappell Clayton are as follows:

1. James (Jimmy)
    A. Angela Kay

Children: Christopher Tommy and Ashley Charlene
B. James Kelly

2. Donny
    A. Donny Keith
        Children: Caleb and Isaac
    B. Shanin Kay
        Children: Margaret (Maggie) and Jack

3. Carolyn
    A. Amanda
        Children: Madison
    B. Carrie

4. Ernie
    A. Angie (adopted)
    B. Staci

Jessie had another son, too, with Norma Chappell:

1. Gary
    A. Lisa Marie
        Children: Nicole and Bradley
    B. Carol Renee
        Children: Rachael Noel, Amanda Ann, and Chance Gary

And so the line continues.

Notes

Notes

Notes

Bibliography

1. Ancestry.com. *1810 United States Federal Census* [database on-line]. Provo, UT, USA: Ancestry.com Operations, Inc., 2010. Images reproduced by FamilySearch.

2. Ancesty.com. *1820 United States Federal Census* [database on-line]. Provo, UT, USA: Ancestry.com Operations, Inc., 2010.

3. Ancesty.com. *1830 United States Federal Census* [database on-line]. Provo, UT, USA: Ancestry.com Operations, Inc., 2010.

4. Ancestry.com. *1840 United States Federal Census* [database on-line]. Provo, UT, USA: Ancestry.com Operations, Inc., 2010.

5. Ancestry.com. *1850 United States Federal Census* [database on-line]. Provo, UT, USA: Ancestry.com Operations, Inc., 2009.

6. Ancestry.com. *1880 United States Federal Census* [database on-line]. Provo, UT, USA: Ancestry.com Operations, Inc., 2009.

7. Ancestry.com. *1900 United States Federal Census* [database on-line]. Lehi, UT, USA: Ancestry.com Operations Inc, 2004.

8. Ancestry.com. *1910 United States Federal Census* [database on-line]. Lehi, UT, USA: Ancestry.com Operations Inc, 2006.

9. Ancestry.com. *1920 United States Federal Census* [database on-line]. Provo, UT, USA: Ancestry.com Operations, Inc., 2010.

10. Ancestry.com. *1930 United States Federal Census* [database on-line]. Provo, UT, USA: Ancestry.com Operations Inc., 2002.

11. Ancestry.com. *1940 United States Federal Census* [database on-line]. Provo, UT, USA: Ancestry.com Operations Inc., 2012.

12. Ancestry.com and The Church of Jesus Christ of Latter-day Saints. *1880 United States Federal Census* [database on-line]. Lehi, UT, USA: Ancestry.com Operations Inc, 2010.

13. Ancestry.com. *Illinois, Compiled Census and Census Substitutes Index, 1810-1890* [database on-line]. Provo, UT, USA: Ancestry.com Operations, Inc., 1999.

14. Ancestry.com. *Kentucky, U.S., Compiled Census and Census Substitutes Index, 1810-1890* [database on-line]. Provo, UT, USA: Ancestry.com Operations Inc, 1999.

15. Ancestry.com. *Kentucky, U.S., County Marriage Records, 1783-1965* [database on-line]. Lehi, UT, USA: Ancestry.com Operations, Inc., 2016.

16. Ancestry.com. *Missouri, U.S., Marriage Records, 1805-2002* [database on-line]. Provo, UT, USA: Ancestry.com Operations, Inc., 2007.

17. Ancestry.com. *North Carolina, U.S., Land Grant Files, 1693-1960* [database on-line]. Provo, UT, USA: Ancestry.com Operations, Inc., 2016.

18. Ancestry.com. *North Carolina Deed Books 1792-1825* [database on-line]. Provo, UT, USA: Ancestry.com Operations Inc, 2006.

19. Ancestry.com. *U.S., Army Indian Campaign Service Records Index, 1815-1858* [database on-line]. Lehi, UT, USA: Ancestry.com Operations Inc, 2017.

20. Ancestry.com. *U.S., Quaker Meeting Records, 1681-1935* [database on-line]. Provo, UT, USA: Ancestry.com Operations, Inc., 2014.

21. Bellarts, James E. *A Genealogy of Clayton, Reynolds, Beals, Brown and Descended and Related Lines.* Portland, Or.: J.E. Bellarts, 1973.

22. Boddie, John Bennett. *Historical Southern Families.* Redwood City, Calif.: Pacific Coast Publishers, 1957.

23. Brashears, Mel. *Mel Brashears' Genealogy.* Available from http://www.melsgenealogy.com/Directory/home.html.

24. "Carolinas." *Wikipedia.* Wikimedia Foundation, 6 Jan. 2021. https://en.wikipedia.org/wiki/Carolinas.

25. "Clayton Hall." *Wikipedia.* Wikimedia Foundation, 2 Dec. 2020, en.wikipedia.org/wiki/Clayton_Hall.

26. "Clayton History, Family Crest & Coats of Arms." *House of Names.* Available from https://www.houseof-names.com/clayton-family-crest#:~:text=The%20Clayton%20Motto%20%20%2B&text=Motto%20Translation%3A%20Probity%20rather%20than%20riches.

27. "Clayton Surname Meaning, History, and Origin." *Select Surnames Website.* Available from https://selectsurnames.com/clayton/.

28. Crozier, William Armstrong. *Virginia Heraldica: being a registry of Virginia gentry entitled to coat armor, with*

genealogical notes of the families. New York, The Genealogical Association, 1908.

29. Dugdale, William, Esq. *The Visitation of the County of York.* London, Blackwood and Sons, Edinburgh, 1666.

30. "Family Coat of Arms and Crests Explained-My Lineage." *MyLineage*, 11 Sept. 2020, www.mylineage.com/family-coat-of-arms-explanation/.

31. "FAQs: heraldry." *College of Arms.* Available from https://www.college-of-arms.gov.uk/resources/faqs#:~:text=A.%20No.,of%20arms%20belong%20to%20individuals.

32. Farrer, William & Brownbill, J. (Eds.) *The Victoria History of the County of Lancaster*, Vol. 6. London, Constable and Company Limited, 1911.

33. Fearnback, Heather. *The Bethania Freedmen's Community.* Winston-Salem, Forsyth County Historic Resources Commission, 2012.

34. Genealogytrails.com. 2021. *History Of Orangeburg, Orangeburg County, SC.* [online] Available at: http://genealogytrails.com/scar/orangeburg/history2.htm.

35. "General Land Office Records." *U.S. Department of the Interior Bureau of Land Management.* Available from https://glorecords.blm.gov/details/patent/default.aspx?accession=0737-243&docClass=MW&sid=sfberfjw.zkg.

36. "1732 John Gowen m. Lettice Winn Bearden in 1759 in Spartanburg Co, SC." *Goyen Family Tree.* Available from https://goyengoinggowengoyneandgone.com/1736-john-buck-gowen-m-lettice-winn-bearden-in-1759-in-spartanburg-county-sc/.

37. Hepburn, Henry F. *The Historical Society of Delaware*. Wilmington, The Historical Society of Delaware, 1904.

38. "Heraldic Meanings." *The American College of Heraldry – Symbolism*. www.americancollegeofheraldry.org/achsymbols.html.

39. *Historical and Biographical Papers*, Volume 4, Issues 34-42. Publication Fund of The Historical Society of Delaware, Wilmington. 1902.

40. Hodgson-Hinde, John. *A History of Northumberland in Three Parts*, Vol. 2-3. Newcastle, 1840.

41. James, G. Watson (Ed.). *Sons of the Revolution in State of Virginia Quarterly Magazine*, Volumes 1-2. January, 1922.

42. Jerome, Brenda Joyce. "Business Partnership – 1816." *Western Kentucky Genealogy Blog.* October 10, 2015. Available from http://wkygenealogy.blogspot.com/search/label/Clayton.

43. Jerome, Brenda Joyce. "Caldwell County Ky Court Order Book B 1815-1818." *Western Kentucky Genealogy Blog*. Available from http://genealogytrails.com/ken/caldwell/caldwell-county-court-order-book-b.html.

44. Jerome, Brenda Joyce. "Obtaining a Tavern License in Early Kentucky." *Western Genealogy Blog*. September 10, 2015. Available from http://wkygenealogy.blogspot.com/2015/09/obtaining-tavern-license-in-early.html.

45. Lamb Family. *Descendants of Thomas Lamb*. [from the records of Cecil Shipley] on sites.rootsweb.com: https://sites.rootsweb.com/~kithandkin2000/lambfamily.htm.

46. "Little River township, Pemiscot County, Missouri (MO) detailed profile." *City-Data.com.* Available at http://www.city-data.com/township/Little-River-Pemiscot-MO.html.

47. McKown, Bryan F., and Michael E. Stauffer. "Destroyed County Records in South Carolina, 1785-1872." *The South Carolina Historical Magazine*, Vol. 97, No. 2, 1996, pp. 149–158. *JSTOR*, www.jstor.org/stable/27570153. Accessed 4 Feb. 2021.

48. *Missouri Death Certificates, 1910-1969.* Available at https://s1.sos.mo.gov/Records/Archives/ArchivesMvc/DeathCertificates/SearchResults).

49. "Muster Roll of the Regiment in Granville County under the Command of Col. William Eaton as taken at a General Muster of the said Regiment 8th October 1754." Granville County North Carolina. Available from http://www.ncgenweb.us/ncgranville/rev/1754-militia.htm.

50. Palmer, Bruce. "Back from the Ashes." *Missouri Conservationist Magazine*. Missouri Department of Conservation, September 2000. Available from https://mdc.mo.gov/conmag/2000/09/back-ashes.

51. Parker, James. *A Glossary of Terms Used in Heraldry*. First publication 1894. Available now at Heraldsnet.org: www.heraldsnet.org/saitou/parker/index.htm.

52. Powell, William S. (Ed.). *Encyclopedia of North Carolina.* University of North Carolina Press, 2006.

53. "Proceedings of the Visitors of William and Mary College, 1716." *The Virginia Magazine of History and Biography*, Vol. 4, No. 2, 1896, pp. 161–175. JSTOR, www.jstor.org/stable/4241948. Accessed 29 Dec. 2020.

54. Putnam, Bill. *The Clayton Family: The Branch from England to America*. Personal Papers, 2009.

55. Rafferty, Milton. "The Ozark Forest: Its Exploitation and Restoration." *OzarksWatch*, Vol. VI, No. 1, 1992, Springfield-Greene County Library.

56. Rayes, N. (n.d.). *Ancestry*. Retrieved January 25, 2021, from https://genetics.thetech.org/ask-a-geneticist/how-far-back-can-ancestry-test-go#:~:text=While%20this%20is%20great%20for,after%20only%20about%20five%20generations.

57. "Record and Image Search." *South Carolina Department of Archives History*. Available from http://www.archivesindex.sc.gov/.

58. "Revolutionary War Soldiers for NC and SC." *OurFamTree.org*. Available from https://www.our-famtree.org/soldier/search.php?state=&fname=&lname=Clayton&rank=&regiment=&keywords=&btn=Search.

59. "Rollo." *Wikipedia*. Wikimedia Foundation, 6 Jan. 2021, en.wikipedia.org/wiki/Rollo.

60. Sarrett, Paul Jr. *Some Early South Carolina Marriage Records: 1641-1799*. Available from http://files.usgwarchives.net/sc/marriages/sc-g1800.txt.

61. "Southern Tobacco in the Civil War." *Shotguns Home of the American Civil War*, 03-09-02. Available from https://civilwarhome.com/tobacco.html.

62. "The Black Hawk War." *Wikipedia*, Wikimedia Foundation, 4 Feb., 2021, https://en.wikipedia.org/wiki/Black_Hawk_War.

63. Toresby, Ralph. *Ducatus Leodiensis, Or, The Topography of the Ancient and Populous Town and Parish of Leedes, And Parts Adjacent in the West-Riding of the County of York.* London, 1715.

64. Tyler, Lyon Gardiner. (Ed.) *Encyclopedia of Virginia Biography*, Vol. 4. New York, Lewis Historical Publishing Company, 1915.

65. Tyler, Lyon G. "Notes by the Editor." *The William and Mary Quarterly*, Vol. 2, No. 4, 1894, pp. 230–236. JSTOR, www.jstor.org/stable/1915403. Accessed 9 Jan. 2021.

66. Underwood, Peter. *Ghosts of North-west England.* Fontana Paperbacks, 1798.

67. "United States General Index to Pension Files, 1861-1934," [database with images]. *FamilySearch* (https://familysearch.org/ark:/61903/3:1:33SQ-GTBJ-98FN?cc=1919699&wc=9FFP-3TL%3A212609001 : 22 May 2014).

68. "Wade Tucker Shot By Jesse Byrd at Peach Orchard." *The Democrat-Argus*. July 23, 1940. Available from https://www.newspapers.com/clip/17014195/the-democrat-argus/.

69. Yates Publishing. *U.S. and International Marriage Records, 1560-1900* [database on-line]. Provo, UT, USA: Ancestry.com Operations Inc, 2004.

Milton Keynes UK
Ingram Content Group UK Ltd.
UKHW051553050424
440686UK00015B/54